——Find——
FREE
——Money for——
Graduate School

Author of FREE Tuition Colleges
Shay Spivey, BSW, MSW

Find FREE Money for Graduate School

By
Shay Spivey, BSW, MSW

Copyright © 2016 Shay Mays

Every effort has been made to ensure that the information contained is valid, truthful, up-to-date, and correct at time of publication. However, by the time this book is published, some of the information may have changed. The author makes no warranty to the accuracy, applicability, or completeness of said information. By reading this book, you acknowledge that you will not hold the author liable for any loss or other damages that may occur.

This is a guide. By reading this book you acknowledge that submitting an application does not guarantee admission or an award. Winners are chosen at the discretion of the individual entities.

Layout: Shay Mays
Cover Design: McLabz Solutions
Photography: Verona Hood-Robinson
Printed in the United States of America

...Dare to Dream

Table of Contents

Brief Summary

Do you need free money to attend graduate school? Not sure where to begin?

I have been there!

Thank you for taking the time to read my book - **Find FREE Money for Graduate School** - and congratulations on your decision to search for alternative ways to pay for graduate school!

I was awarded over $100,000 in college scholarships and free financial aid as an adult student and single parent. I attended graduate school full time and graduated with honors. As a scholarship winner and college graduate, I am devoted to helping others find, apply, and win free money to further their education.

This easy guide will show you how to **Find FREE Money for Graduate School** – Scholarships, fellowships, and much more.

This is not a scholarship directory. However, I do provide a list of helpful books and directories.

Other Books by Shay Spivey

How to Submit a Winning Scholarship
Application: Secret Techniques I Used to Win
$100,000 in College Scholarships (2014)

How to Find Scholarships and Free Financial Aid
for Private High Schools (2015)

FREE Tuition Colleges 2016 (2016)

FREE Tuition Colleges for Adults 50+ (2016)

Find FREE Money for Graduate School (2016)

About the Author

Author and Social Worker, Shay Spivey, was awarded over $100,000 in college scholarships to fund her college education as an adult student and single parent. Shay received her Bachelor and Master of Social Work from Indiana University.

Today, the Scholarship Advisor Program founder has written several books that show students and families how to access free money for education.

In an effort to pay it forward, Shay teaches scholarship workshops in partnership with schools and organizations that help disadvantaged student's access education.

Introduction

If you cannot afford to pay for a graduate degree, then this guide if for you! **Find Free Money for Graduate School** is a great resource for college students and future college students looking for ways to pay for graduate school outside of student loans.

Many college students want to further their education with a graduate or doctorate degree but simply cannot afford the cost of tuition. Scholarships and free financial aid are the solution, and they help students eliminate the financial barriers that prevent access to higher education. But what other FREE money options are available?

Find Free Money for Graduate School provides information about how to find free financial aid for graduate and doctorate programs.

Earning an undergraduate degree is expensive, but a graduate degree costs even more. I want everyone to know that scholarships and free financial aid do exist for educational opportunities beyond your first degree.

Find Free Money for Graduate School was written to take the mystery out of where to locate these funds.

Inside this guide I provide you with a good description of the various types of graduate school funding options available for graduate studies – scholarships, fellowships, and much more.

This is not a scholarship directory. However, I do provide a list of helpful books and directories.

Graduation School is Expensive

The average cost of master's degree for students is between $20,000 and $120,000. The costs vary depending on the university and the master's program itself.

The student loan debt crisis has reached over one trillion dollars in the U.S. Unfortunately, student loans are often the only form of financial aid that most graduate students are aware of. However, there are alternative FREE ways to meet the tuition costs of a graduate program.

They DO Exist!
Contrary to popular belief, free money is available to help students pursue a master's' or doctorate degree, and pay tuition, fees, and living expenses. You just need to know where to look.

Competition
Graduate school is competitive and so is financial aid. Unfortunately, most students miss out on free money because they are not aware of the opportunities.

Good Grades are Important

It is important to note that when transitioning from undergraduate to graduate school, academics count the most, and consideration for financial aid is no exception. The better your grades are the better your chances of qualifying for financial aid opportunities.

Let's get started...

Where Do I Start?

Applying for scholarships and free financial aid takes organization, work, and time - just like applying to graduate school. Following are a few tips and techniques that will be helpful in your search.

Start Early

Start the process of searching for and applying to financial aid opportunities at least one year to six months in advance. The majority of funding decisions are made early, however sometimes last-minute funding becomes available.

Apply to More than One Program

Many students apply to several graduate schools and compare financial aid packages offered by each of the programs before making a decision. To keep your options open and avoid missing deadlines, you should move quickly to accept the financial aid packages from each school that offers one. After you choose a school, send a courteous decline letter to the other programs so they can release the funds to another student.

University Graduate Office

Contact the university graduate admissions or dean's office and ask about any opportunities available for graduate studies. Also, when you submit your application for admission, be sure to mark the section on the application that asks if you need funding.

The Graduate School

Ask your graduate school advisor or any department faculty that can be of assistance for help in finding free money. If one person does not have an answer, ask the next person. Someone knows about available funding and this is not the time to be shy - be polite but not shy.

College Research Institutes and Centers

College Research Institutes and Centers lead the way in research development and scholarly activity. They set aside funding for graduate students each school year. You will want to seek out these highly competitive opportunities well in advance.

18

Important Terms

A few of the terms used when describing graduate school funding are different than undergraduate financial aid. Following are terms often used to describe the type of aid provided by different types of awards. It will be helpful to know their definitions.

Stipend: A stipend is a fixed payment similar to an earned salary or wage. Graduate students can earn stipends by teaching or doing research for a faculty member.

Tuition Waiver: A reduction in tuition. In place of awarding a scholarship, colleges will not bill for all or part of a student's tuition.

Scholarship Awards

Scholarships are free financial aid that is awarded to individuals pursuing a college degree and do not have to be repaid. Free money!

Types of Scholarships

-*Merit-based scholarships* are based on a student's academic, artistic, athletic or other abilities.

-*Need-based scholarships* are based on the student and family's financial record and may require the student to fill out a Free Application for Federal Student Aid (FAFSA) in order to qualify.

-*Student-specific scholarships* are given to applicants that identify with a specific group (gender, race, religion, family and medical history, etc.).

-*Career-specific scholarships* are awarded by a college or university awards to students who plan to pursue a specific field of study.

-College-specific scholarships are offered by individual colleges and universities to highly qualified applicants based on academic and personal achievement or personal circumstances.

Where to Locate Scholarships

There are multiple ways to find scholarships. Though the number of opportunities available decrease at the graduate level, they DO exist! Following are the sources that are proven to be helpful in searching for free money for graduate school.

Library

Your Local Library is a wealth of FREE resources. Scholarship seekers should spend time at the library researching and reading about scholarships and financial aid. Ask the staff about college resources - they love to help.

FREE Websites - Free Online Scholarship Matching Services

Free online scholarship matching services are a great way to find free money for college. These online databases help you find free scholarships that match your criteria. After completing a profile, the search engine will continuously search for any opportunities that fit YOUR characteristics.

www.fastweb.com
www.scholarships.com

College Financial Aid Office

The college financial aid office is the hub of all financial aid activity; all financial transactions go through them (including student loans). The majority of all colleges have a financial aid website that you can visit. Make an appointment with a financial aid officer today.

College Scholarship Office

Most people are not aware that colleges have a scholarship office (separate from the financial aid office). The scholarship office is one of your most valuable resources for finding free money. Opportunities such as college-based scholarships are often offered through the college of your choice. Also, the scholarship office can provide a list of available scholarship opportunities from the college and the community.

Community Service

Community Service wins scholarships! Many schools offer scholarship money to students that commit to volunteering a certain number of hours to non-profit agencies. Contact your individual college community service office or scholarship office to find out more about these opportunities.

Religious Organizations

If you are affiliated with a religious group, make sure you contact them and ask about any scholarship opportunities they offer.

Business and Professional Organizations

What is your field of interest? Most career fields are supported by either a business or professional organization, and these organizations often provide scholarships. A quick online search will start you off in the right direction. For example, if you want to be a teacher, do an internet search for "professional organizations for teachers." If want to attend law school, search for "professional organizations for lawyers."

Charities and Nonprofit Organizations

Many charities and non-profit organizations provide graduate funding in their specific fields such as the sciences, education, and languages.

Sample List of Scholarships

Following is a sample list of graduate scholarships. In the **Resource** section at the end of this book, you'll find a list of scholarships for graduate schools:

Alpha Kappa Alpha Educational Advancement Foundation, Inc.

The Alpha Kappa Alpha Educational Advancement Foundation provides one-year, one-time-only scholarships to graduate students.
Website: www.akaeaf.org

Astronaut Scholarship in Science and Technology

The Astronaut Scholarship in Science and Technology is open to students majoring in engineering, natural science, applied science, or mathematics.
Website: astronautscholarship.org

Congressional Black Caucus Foundation (CBCF) - Spouses Education Scholarship

The Congressional Black Caucus Foundation (CBCF) provides scholarships for students of all majors who are applying to or currently

participating in an undergraduate or graduate
degree program at an accredited U.S. college or
university.
Website: www.cbcfinc.org

D.J. Lovell Scholarship
The D.J. Lovell Scholarship is open to full-time
undergraduate and graduate students who are
studying optical science and engineering.
Website: spie.org

Dr. Nancy Foster Scholarship Program
The Dr. Nancy Foster Scholarship Program is
available to graduate-level students, particularly
females and minorities, who are interested in
independent research in oceanography, marine
biology, or maritime archaeology.
Website: fosterscholars.noaa.gov

Health Professions Scholarship Program
The Health Professions Scholarship Program
from the U.S. Army Medical Department is open
to full-time students enrolled in a graduate-level
health care degree program in the U.S. or Puerto
Rico. To qualify, applicants should check
enlistment requirements.
Website: www.goarmy.com

University of Pennsylvania Law School - Levy Scholars Program Scholarship

The Levy Scholars Program Scholarship is available to entering students at the University of Pennsylvania Law School.
Website: www.law.upenn.edu

LexisNexis/John R. Johnson Memorial Scholarship

The LexisNexis/John R. Johnson Memorial Scholarship is open to individuals who plan to pursue graduate-level studies related to their professional interests in law librarianship.
Website: www.aallnet.org

Ralph Johnson Bunche Distinguished Graduate Scholarship

The Ralph Johnson Bunche Distinguished Graduate Scholarship is available to full-time entering students at Rutgers University, School of Law, Newark.
Website: law.newark.rutgers.edu

University of Pennsylvania Law School - Dean's Scholarship

The Dean's Scholarship is available to students at the University of Pennsylvania Law School.
Website: www.law.upenn.edu

Grants

Grants are a great FREE option for paying for graduate school. There are multiple free grant databases available to assist graduate and postgraduate students in finding grants.

Grants can come from government agencies, corporations, charities, professional organizations, universities, non-profits, and individuals.

Some grant opportunities are large and some are small. But free money is free money and it all adds up.

For example, there are grants for people who belong to a specific organization like the Girl Scouts of America. There are also grants for single parents and women returning to school after a period of time.

Where do you start? The library is an excellent place to start your search for grants! You can usually access grant databases for free through the public library. Also, there is a great list of grant directories in the resource section of this book.

Fellowships

What are Fellowships?
Fellowships are free financial aid and are granted to individuals pursuing a college graduate degree as a form of merit-based financial aid, similar to a scholarship. These awards are based on academic achievements or research goals. Fellowships are considered to be prestigious and very competitive.

Eligibility requirements, award amounts, and length of fellowship may vary. In addition, tuition waivers are available to students appointed to a fellowship. There are many types of fellowships, including but not limited to: research fellowships, teaching fellowships, honorary fellowships, and medical/health fellowships.

What is Included?
Fellowships can include a variety of incentives such as:

-Tuition waivers
-Monthly stipends
-Health insurance
-Dental insurance

-Travel funds
-Faculty support

Where to Look
Learn more about available fellowships in your field through your academic departments, private organizations, government grant sites, and free online scholarship databases.

Sample List of Fellowships

American Psychological Association Minority Fellowship Program

The American Psychological Association Minority Fellowship Program helps graduate students, postdoctoral trainees and early career professionals in areas related to ethnic minority psychology.
Website: www.apa.org/pi/mfp/

American Sociological Association Minority Fellowship Program

The American Sociological Association Minority Fellowship Program supports the development and training of sociologists of color in any sub-area or specialty in the discipline.
Website: www.asanet.org/funding/mfp.cfm

ASEE/NSF Small Business Postdoctoral Research Diversity Fellowship

The ASEE/NSF Small Business Postdoctoral Research Diversity Fellowship is available to recent engineering PhD's who are pursuing an opportunity to conduct research in a corporate setting.

Fellows must hold a PhD awarded in a S.T.E.M. field within the last seven years to be considered. Website: nsfsbir.asee.org

Congressional Black Caucus Foundation (CBCF) - Fellowship

The Congressional Black Caucus Foundation (CBCF) provides fellowships for students completing a graduate degree program. Website: www.cbcfinc.org

PIRG Fellowship

The PIRG Fellowship is available to recent college graduates who are interested in the public interest movement. Website: jobs.uspirg.org

William Randolph Hearst Endowed Fellowship for Minority Students

The William Randolph Hearst Endowed Fellowship for Minority Students is available to minority undergraduate and graduate students with a background in the social sciences or humanities. Website: www.aspeninstitute.org

Pedro Zamora Public Policy Fellowship

The Public Policy Fellowship is open to young professionals, undergraduate and graduate

students who seek experience in HIV-related public policy and government affairs.
Website: www.aidsunited.org

National Gallery of Art Conservation Fellowship

The National Gallery of Art Conservation Fellowship is open to art conservation graduate students with no more than five years of work experience who are interested in the examination and treatment of works of art.
Website: www.nga.gov

Webb Family Graduate Fellowship in Oceanography

The Webb Family Graduate Fellowship in Oceanography is available to graduate oceanography majors at the University of Rhode Island.
Website: www.uri.edu

Intel PhD Fellowship Program

The Intel PhD Fellowship Program is open to PhD candidates at select U.S. universities who are working in fields related to Intel's business and research interests.
Website: www.intel.com

Swann Foundation Fellowship

The Swann Foundation Fellowship is available to graduate students who are conducting scholarly research and writing projects in the field of caricature and cartoon.

Website: www.loc.gov/rr/print/swann/swann-fellow.html

Western Civilization Fellowship

The Western Civilization Fellowship is available for graduate dissertation work related to Western Civilizations.

Website: home.isi.org/students/fellowships

Assistantships

Assistantships require students to work for the university in various capacities. They provide an opportunity for graduates to focus on their studies, acquire valuable professional experience, and work closely with faculty. Assistantship awards often include a stipend, tuition waiver, and health insurance. Tuition waivers are often available to students appointed to an assistantship. Following are examples of types of assistantships:

Graduate Assistant
A graduate assistantship position provides a tuition waiver to eligible graduate students in exchange for working part-time and providing support to professors and/or doctoral students.

Teaching Assistant
A graduate teaching assistantship position provides a stipend and/or tuition waiver to eligible graduate and postgraduate students in exchange for a commitment to teach part time and/or provide assistance to a professor.

Research Assistant
A graduate assistantship position provides a tuition waiver to eligible graduate students in exchange for academic research support. Research assistantships provide research-related learning activities along with financial support.

How exciting would it be to work side by side with a professor on an important research project?

Adjunct Faculty Position

Adjunct Faculty are part-time or contingent college professors that are not eligible for tenure. This position provides tuition waivers to eligible graduate students in exchange for teaching and research commitments. For more information contact the graduate program director.

Travel Grants

Travel grant awards are available to help graduate and postgraduate students fund travel expenses to conferences, trainings, professional meetings, and presentations.

Employer Educational Benefits

Do you work for a company that offers educational benefits?

Educational benefits from an employer can include payments for tuition, fees, books, supplies, and equipment. In the same way, some employers offer tuition reimbursement to their employees. Eligibility requirements will vary and may depend on full-time or part time employment.

Following are a few companies that will help pay your graduate school tuition:

-AT&T provides tuition aid, up to $5,250 annually for courses leading up to an approved undergraduate or graduate degree. Learn more at: att.jobs

-Ford has an Education Tuition Assistance Plan that provides up to $5,000 a year for courses leading to an associates, bachelors, master's degree, or Ph.D. Learn more at: uawford.org/edtp/etap

-**Wells Fargo** will reimburse you for eligible tuition expenses up to $5,000 annually.
Learn more at:
www.wellsfargo.com/about/careers/benefits

University Employment

One of the advantages of working for a college is reduced or free tuition. Be sure to check your college websites for potential job opportunities.

Universities offer a wide variety of employment opportunities to graduate students to help pay educational expenses. Students can work for their departments or find internships. Graduate students should seek academic employment opportunities through their department or programs.

College Resident Assistant Positions
Colleges with dormitories and other types of on-campus housing often hire students for resident assistant positions. A resident assistant (RA) is a trained peer leader who oversees students living in college housing facilities. There are many benefits to being an RA, and the incentive package may vary by schools. Some colleges offer free room and board, while others may provide scholarships, tuition discounts, stipends, free parking and/or a paycheck in exchange for your services.

47

To learn more, contact the college of your choice and ask about resident assistant opportunities.

Free Master's Program

Free graduate programs are almost unheard of, but at least one of these rare educational opportunities exists.

The Wake Forest University School of Business offers a full-tuition scholarship award to the Masters of Art degree for minority students. In addition to tuition, the award also includes a stipend to help cover living expenses and a high-level executive personal mentor.

Attention: Corporate Fellowship Program
Wake Forest University School of Business
Master of Arts in Management
1834 Wake Forest Road
Winston-Salem, NC 27106
Phone: 866-925-3622
Learn more
at: business.wfu.edu/corporatefellow

Think International

Have you considered studying abroad? If so, consider applying to the following prestigious scholarship awards that support international studies.

Fulbright U.S. Student Program

Description: The Fulbright U.S. Student Program provides grants for individually designed study/research projects or for English Teaching Assistant Programs during one academic year in a participating country outside the U.S. It is open to masters and doctoral candidates. Grant benefits for all Fulbright U.S. Student grants include round-trip transportation to the host country, room, board, and health benefits.
Website: us.fulbrightonline.org

Marshall Scholarships

Description: Marshall Scholarships finance young Americans of high ability to study for a graduate degree in the United Kingdom.
Website: www.marshallscholarship.org

Rhodes Scholarships

Description: A Rhodes Scholarship provides tuition, fees, and additional costs for graduate work at Oxford University located in the United Kingdom.

Website: www.rhodesscholar.org

Rotary Global Grants

Description: Rotary Global Grants support scholarships for graduate-level academic studies that support large international activities with sustainable, measurable outcomes in the Rotary's areas of focus.

Website: www.rotary.org

Watson Fellowship

Description: This program provides $25,000 for one year of independent research and travel outside the United States. You must be a senior graduating from a participating U.S. college.

Website: watson.foundation

Avoid Scams

Thousands of students are victims of scholarship scams every year. The expense of college causes a lot of stress over how to pay for it. Now that you know where to find free money for graduate school, it is important to know how to spot a scholarship scam. Following are several common scams used to swindle people out of their hard earned money.

Never Pay to Apply for a Scholarship
Legitimate scholarships never charge applicants to apply. There are no application, registration, processing or administrative fees. If you are asked to pay to apply that is a red flag that the "scholarship" may be a scam. Never pay to apply for or receive a scholarship.

Never Give Out Your Financial Information
If a scholarship organization or representative asks you for credit card or bank account information - refuse. This information is not necessary to award a scholarship. Most scholarship money is mailed directly to your college financial aid office and applied directly to your student account. Any excess funds are distributed to you by the school.

Beware of statements like:
"To hold this scholarship for you, please provide your bank account number or credit card information."

"This scholarship is guaranteed or your money back!"

Avoid Guarantees for a Fee
Real scholarship opportunities never ask for a fee to apply nor do they guarantee you will win just for applying. "Guarantees" are a red flag that this may be a scam.

Summary

Thank you for taking the time to read my book. Now you know where to **Find FREE Money for Graduate School!**

Scholarships
Grants
Fellowships
Assistantships
Adjunct Faculty Positions
Travel Grants
Employer Education Benefits
University Employment
Free Graduate Program
Study Abroad Opportunities

The Next Step is Up to You

Good luck on your search to **Find FREE Money for Graduate School**. I hope this information gets you one step closer to achieving your educational goals. Knowledge is power!

Now that you know about **Find FREE Money for Graduate School** what will you do with the information? My graduate degree was paid for and I want the same for you. GO FOR IT!

Resources

Free Online Scholarship Matching Services

FastWeb

FastWeb helps thousands of students pay for school by matching them to scholarships, grants and awards for which they qualify.
Website: www.fastweb.com

Scholarship.com

Scholarship.com is a free scholarship matching website that connects students to thousands of financial aid opportunities.
Website: www.scholarships.com

Most Generous and Competitive Graduate Scholarships and Fellowships

Alfred P. Sloan Foundation Research Fellowships

The Sloan Research Fellowships provide support to young scientists and research faculty in physics, chemistry, mathematics, neuroscience, economics, computer science, and computational and evolutionary molecular biology.
Website: www.sloan.org/sloan-research-fellowships

Beinecke Scholarship Program

The Beinecke Scholarship Program is open to college juniors who intend to pursue graduate study in the arts, humanities, or social sciences at any accredited university.
Website: fdnweb.org/beinecke

Boren Fellowships

Boren Fellowships provide up to $30,000 to U.S. graduate students to add an important international and language component to their graduate education through specialization in area study, language study, or increased language proficiency. Boren Fellowships support

study and research in areas of the world that are critical to U.S. interests, including Africa, Asia, Central & Eastern Europe, Eurasia, Latin America, and the Middle East. The countries of Western Europe, Canada, Australia, and New Zealand are excluded.
Website: www.borenawards.org

Davies-Jackson Scholarship
The Davies-Jackson Scholarship provides support for a two-year course of study at St. John's College, Cambridge University. Fields of study include Archaeology and Anthropology, Classics, Economics, English, Geography, History, History of Art, Modern and Medieval Languages, Music, Philosophy, and Social and Political Sciences.
Website: www.cic.edu

EPA Science to Achieve Results (STAR) Fellowship Program for Graduate Environmental Study
The Environmental Protection Agency's STAR Fellowship Program provides graduate fellowships for master and doctoral students pursuing degrees in environmental fields.
Website: www.epa.gov/research-fellowships

Ford Foundation Predoctoral Fellowships for Minorities
The Ford Foundation Predoctoral Fellowships for Minorities program provides graduate fellowships for research-based PhD or ScD students in Archaeology, Anthropology, Art History, Astronomy, Chemistry, Communications, Computer Science, Earth Sciences, Economics, Engineering, Ethnomusicology, Geography, History, International Relations, Life Sciences, Linguistics, Literature, Language, Mathematics, Performance Study, Philosophy, Physics, Political Science, Psychology, Religion, Sociology, and Urban Planning.
Website: sites.nationalacademies.org/pga/fordf ellowships

Fulbright Fellowships
Graduate Fulbright Fellowships are for US citizens to study in other countries and for international students to study in the US. US students must apply through their campus Fulbright program advisor.
Website: www.iie.org/fulbright

Gates Cambridge Scholarships

The Gates Cambridge Scholarships are open to graduate students from outside the United Kingdom for study at the University of Cambridge.
Website: www.gatescambridge.org

Harry S. Truman Scholarships

The Harry S. Truman Scholarships are open to college juniors who are US citizens and nationals and who want to go to graduate school in preparation for a career in public service.
Website: www.truman.gov

Henry Luce Foundation Scholarship

The Luce Scholarships provide stipends and internships for Americans to live and work in Asia each year. Candidates must be US citizens who have earned a bachelor's degree and are less than 30 years old.
Website: www.hluce.org

Hertz Foundation Graduate Fellowships in Applied Physical Sciences

The Hertz Foundation Graduate Fellowships are awarded to graduate students who are expected to have the greatest impact on the application of the physical sciences to human problems.
Website: hertzfoundation.org

IBM PhD Fellowships

IBM PhD Fellowships are available to PhD students in business, chemistry, computer science, electrical engineering, materials science, mathematics, mechanical engineering and physics, as well as a variety of emerging technical fields.
Website:
www.research.ibm.com/university/awards/phd fellowship.shtml

Jacob K. Javits Fellowship Programs

The Jacob K. Javits Graduate Fellowships support graduate students in the arts, humanities and social sciences.
Website:
www2.ed.gov/programs/jacobjavits/index.html

James Madison Graduate Fellowships

The James Madison Fellowships are open to college seniors and recent college graduates who intend to go to graduate school on a full-time basis. The fellowships provide funding for a master's degree at any accredited institution of higher education in the United States. Candidates must intend to become secondary school teachers of American history, American government and social studies.
Website: www.jamesmadison.gov

Marshall Scholarships
The Marshall Sherfield Scholarships Program is a highly competitive program in which young Americans are chosen to pursue a graduate education in the United Kingdom each year. The awards cover two years of study at any British university.
Website: www.marshallscholarship.org

Morris K. Udall Foundation Environmental Public Policy and Conflict Resolution PhD Fellowships
The Morris K. Udall Foundation awards PhD dissertation fellowships to graduate students in the areas of environmental public policy or environmental conflict resolution.
Website: www.udall.gov

George Mitchell Scholarships
The George Mitchell Scholarships are awarded to American students to pursue one year of postgraduate study at an Ireland university.
Website: www.us-irelandalliance.org

Link Foundation Energy Fellowship Program
The Link Foundation Energy Fellowship Program provides an annual stipend for PhD students in the area of societal production and utilization of energy.
Website: www.linkenergy.org

NASA Graduate Student Researchers Program (GSRP)
The NASA Graduate Student Researchers Program (GSRP) provides fellowships for graduate study leading to a master's or doctoral degree in science, mathematics or engineering.
Website: www.nasa.gov

National Defense Science and Engineering Graduate Fellowship
The National Defense Science and Engineering Graduate Fellowships support graduate students pursuing a doctoral degree in Aeronautical and Astronautical Engineering; Biosciences; Chemical Engineering; Chemistry; Civil Engineering; Cognitive, Neural; and Behavioral Sciences Computer and Computational Sciences; Electrical Engineering; Geosciences; Materials Science and Engineering; Mathematics; Mechanical Engineering; Naval Architecture and Ocean Engineering; Oceanography and Physics.
Website: ndseg.asee.org

National Physical Science Consortium

The National Physical Science Consortium (NPSC) sponsors a graduate fellowship program for graduate students pursuing a PhD in the physical sciences at participating colleges and universities. Fields of study include Astronomy, Chemistry, Computer Science, Geology, Materials Science, Mathematical Sciences, Physics, and related engineering fields, including Chemical, Computer, Electrical, Environmental, and Mechanical Engineering.
Website: www.npsc.org

National Science Foundation Graduate Research Foundation

The U.S. National Science Foundation (NSF) Graduate Research Fellowship provides awards to graduate students in the mathematical, physical, biological, engineering, and behavioral and social sciences. Website: www.nsfgrfp.org

Paul and Daisy Soros Fellowships for New Americans

The Paul and Daisy Soros Fellowships provide for up to two years of graduate study in the US for "New Americans." New Americans include resident aliens, naturalized US citizens, and the children of two parents who are both naturalized US citizens. Fellows may pursue graduate

degrees in any professional field, such as engineering, medicine, law, and social work, or any scholarly discipline in the arts, humanities, social sciences, and sciences.
Website: www.pdsoros.org

Rhodes Scholarship
The Rhodes Scholarships enable students from many countries to study at the University of Oxford.
Website: www.rhodesscholar.org

Social Science Research Council International Dissertation Research Fellowship
The Social Science Research Council International Dissertation Field Research Fellowship (IDRF) program is for graduate students in the humanities and social sciences who are conducting doctoral dissertation field research outside the United States.
Website: www.ssrc.org/programs/idrf

Spencer Foundation Dissertation Fellowships for Research Related to Education
The Spencer Foundation Dissertation Fellowships for Research Related to Education are open to doctoral degree candidates at graduate schools in the United States. The emphasis is on the improvement of education.

Website: www.spencer.org

Wenner-Gren Fellowships

The Wenner-Gren Foundation awards grants for Dissertation Fieldwork for basic research in anthropology.
Website: www.wennergren.org

Winston Churchill Scholarship Foundation

The Churchill Scholarship Program enables young Americans to pursue graduate study in science, mathematics, and engineering at Churchill College, Cambridge University.
Website: www.winstonchurchillfoundation.org

Woodrow Wilson National Fellowship Foundation - Charlotte W. Newcombe Doctoral Dissertation Fellowship

The Charlotte W. Newcombe Doctoral Dissertation Fellowships are for doctoral students who look at the ethical or religious values in all fields of the humanities and social sciences.
Website: woodrow.org/fellowships/newcombe

Woodrow Wilson National Fellowship Foundation - Mellon Foundation Fellowships
The Andrew W. Mellon Fellowships in Humanistic Studies provide support for first-year doctoral students in the humanities.
Website: woodrow.org/fellowships/mellon

Woodrow Wilson National Fellowship Foundation - Thomas R. Pickering Foreign Affairs Fellowship
The Thomas R. Pickering Foreign Affairs Fellowship is designed to attract outstanding individuals from all ethnic, racial, and social backgrounds who have an interest in pursuing a Foreign Service career with the U.S. Department of State.
Website: woodrow.org/fellowships/pickering

Woodrow Wilson National Fellowship Foundation - Woodrow Wilson Dissertation Fellowship in Women's Studies
The Women's Studies Fellowships are provided to Ph.D. candidates with an interest in and commitment to women's issues, at institutions in the United States, and who will complete their dissertations during the fellowship year.
Website: woodrow.org/fellowships/womens-studies

Scholarships for Graduate Students

This is a SHORT list of scholarships that are available to graduate students. There are thousands more out there!

Alpha Kappa Alpha Educational Advancement Foundation, Inc.

The Alpha Kappa Alpha Educational Advancement Foundation provides one-year one-time-only scholarships to graduate students.
Website: www.akaeaf.org/graduate_scholarship
s

Astronaut Scholarship in Science and Technology

The Astronaut Scholarship in Science and Technology is open to students majoring in engineering, natural science, applied science, or mathematics.
Website: astronautscholarship.org

Congressional Black Caucus Foundation (CBCF) - Spouses Education Scholarship

The Congressional Black Caucus Foundation (CBCF) provides scholarships for students of all majors who are applying to or currently participating in an undergraduate or graduate

71

degree program at an accredited U.S. college or university.
Website: www.cbcfinc.org

D.J. Lovell Scholarship

The D.J. Lovell Scholarship is open to full-time undergraduate and graduate students who are studying optical science and engineering.
Website: spie.org

Dr. Nancy Foster Scholarship Program

The Dr. Nancy Foster Scholarship Program is available to graduate-level students, particularly females and minorities, who are interested in independent research in oceanography, marine biology, or maritime archaeology.
Website: fosterscholars.noaa.gov

Health Professions Scholarship Program

The Health Professions Scholarship Program from the U.S. Army Medical Department is open to full-time students enrolled in a graduate-level health care degree program in the U.S. or Puerto Rico.
Website: www.goarmy.com

Levy Scholars Program Scholarship

The Levy Scholars Program Scholarship is available to entering students at the University of Pennsylvania Law School.
Website: www.law.upenn.edu

LexisNexis/John R. Johnson Memorial Scholarship

The LexisNexis/John R. Johnson Memorial Scholarship is open to individuals who plan to pursue graduate-level studies related to their professional interests in law librarianship.
Website: www.aallnet.org

Ralph Johnson Bunche Distinguished Graduate Scholarship

The Ralph Johnson Bunche Distinguished Graduate Scholarship is available to full-time entering students at Rutgers University School of Law - Newark.
Website: law.newark.rutgers.edu

University of Pennsylvania Law School - Dean's Scholarship

The Dean's Scholarship is available to students at the University of Pennsylvania Law School.
Website: www.law.upenn.edu

Fellowships for Graduate Students

This is a SHORT list of fellowships that are available to graduate students. There are thousands more out there!

American Psychological Association Minority Fellowship Program

The American Psychological Association Minority Fellowship Program helps graduate students, postdoctoral trainees and early career professionals in areas related to ethnic minority psychology.
Website: www.apa.org/pi/mfp/

American Sociological Association Minority Fellowship Program

The American Sociological Association Minority Fellowship Program supports the development and training of sociologists of color in any sub-area or specialty in the discipline.
Website: www.asanet.org/funding/mfp.cfm

ASEE/NSF Small Business Postdoctoral Research Diversity Fellowship

The ASEE/NSF Small Business Postdoctoral Research Diversity Fellowship is available to recent engineering PhD's who are pursuing an

opportunity to conduct research in a corporate setting.
Fellows must hold a PhD awarded in a S.T.E.M. field within the last seven years to be considered.
Website: nsfsbir.asee.org

Congressional Black Caucus Foundation (CBCF) - Fellowship

The Congressional Black Caucus Foundation (CBCF) provides fellowships for students completing a graduate degree program.
Website: www.cbcfinc.org

PIRG Fellowship

The PIRG Fellowship is available to recent college graduates who are interested in the public interest movement.
Website: jobs.uspirg.org

William Randolph Hearst Endowed Fellowship for Minority Students

The William Randolph Hearst Endowed Fellowship for Minority Students is available to minority undergraduate and graduate students with a background in the social sciences or humanities.
Website: www.aspeninstitute.org

Pedro Zamora Public Policy Fellowship

The Public Policy Fellowship is open to young professionals, undergraduate and graduate students who seek experience in HIV-related public policy and government affairs.
Website: www.aidsunited.org

National Gallery of Art Conservation Fellowship

The National Gallery of Art Conservation Fellowship is open to art conservation graduate students with no more than five years of work experience who are interested in the examination and treatment of works of art.
Website: www.nga.gov

Webb Family Graduate Fellowship in Oceanography

The Webb Family Graduate Fellowship in Oceanography is available to graduate oceanography majors at the University of Rhode Island.
Website: www.uri.edu

Intel PhD Fellowship Program

The Intel PhD Fellowship Program is open to PhD candidates at select U.S. universities who are working in fields related to Intel's business and research interests.

Website: www.intel.com

Swann Foundation Fellowship

The Swann Foundation Fellowship is available to graduate students who are conducting scholarly research and writing projects in the field of caricature and cartoon.
Website: www.loc.gov/rr/print/swann/swann-fellow.html

Western Civilization Fellowship

The Western Civilization Fellowship is available for graduate dissertation work related to Western Civilizations.
Website: home.isi.org/students/fellowships

Books and Directories - Scholarships and Fellowships for Graduate School

Annual Register of Grant Support: A Directory of Funding Resources, 48th edition (2014)
Edited By McDonough and Bazikian

Assistantships and Graduate Fellowships in the Mathematical Sciences (2011)
By American Mathematical Society

Dan Cassidy's Worldwide Graduate Scholarship Directory: Thousands of Top Scholarships Throughout the United States & Around the World (2000)
By D. Cassidy

Financing Graduate School, 2nd edition (1996)
By P. McWade

Foundation Directory (2016)
By Foundation Center

Foundation Grants to Individuals (1995)
By L. Victoria Hall

Free Money for Graduate School (1993)
By L. Blum

The Grants Register 2013: The Complete Guide to Postgraduate Funding Worldwide (2012)
By P. Macmillan

Getting What You Came For: The Smart Student's Guide to Earning a Master's or Ph.D. (1992)
By R. Peters

The Graduate Student's Complete Scholarship Book (1998)
By Student Services Inc.

Minority Financial Aid Directory (1995)
By L. Berry

Prentice Hall Guide to Scholarships and Fellowships for Math and Science Students (1993)
By Kantrowitz and DiGennaro

Money for Graduate Students in the Humanities (2010)
By Schlacter and Weber

Money for Graduate Students in the Physical & Earth Sciences (2010)
By Schlacter and Weber

Money for Graduate Students in the Social &
Behavioral Sciences (2010)
By Schlacter and Weber

The Ultimate Grad School Survival Guide (1996)
By L. Mitchell

Contact Shay Spivey

Thank you for your purchase! I would love to receive your feedback after you finish reading. Please share your thoughts about this book by leaving a review wherever you made your purchase.

Email: shayspivey@yahoo.com

Blog: scholarshipadvisor.blogspot.com

Blog: shayspivey.blogspot.com

Facebook: www.facebook.com/authorshayspivey

Twitter: @ShayMSpivey

About.me/shay.spivey

Thank you!

Readers!

Keanah, Verona, & Lydia: My lifelong friends and constant source of support, love, and encouragement.

Cherri: My sister, my rock.

Maya & Tylin: My reasons for living.

Education: For opening up my world; introducing me to new things, ideas, opportunities, and experiences.

God: For all your grace, mercy, and favor. For the Journey.

CPSIA information can be obtained
at www.ICGtesting.com
Printed in the USA
LVOW01s0305100816
499772LV00021B/367/P